AMAZING GRACE

·Smith Island and the Chesapeake Watermen·

·written and photographed by Bernard Wolf·

Macmillan Publishing Company   New York
Collier Macmillan Publishers   London

The author wishes to express his sincere gratitude to Mr. Jim Holt, Director of the Chesapeake Bay Maritime Museum, St. Michaels, Maryland, and Miss Elizabeth Hall of Princess Anne and Crisfield, Maryland, for their invaluable assistance. He also wishes to thank Reverends Janet and Bill Rounsley of Ewell, Maryland, as well as all the good people of Smith Island for their genuine courtesy and goodwill.

10 9 8 7 6 5 4 3 2 1

The text of this book is set in 14-point Goudy Old Style.
The illustrations are black-and-white photographs reproduced in halftone.
Library of Congress Cataloging-in-Publication Data. Wolf, Bernard. Amazing grace. Summary: Text and photographs portray life on Smith Island in the Chesapeake Bay, with an emphasis on the traditional activity of crabbing as it is practiced there. 1. Crabbing—Smith Island (Md. and Va.)—Juvenile literature. 2. Smith Island (Md. and Va.)—Social life and customs—Juvenile literature. [1. Crabbing—Smith Island (Md. and Va.) 2. Smith Island (Md. and Va.)—Social life and customs] I. Title.
SH400.5.C7W65   1986   975.5'18   86-8227   ISBN 0-02-793330-X

For William Warner,
whose *Beautiful Swimmers* inspired this book,
and for Barbara Dize,
who took in a stranger and made him welcome.

The sun rises, pink and bloated, with the promise of heat and suffering for those on land. But here there is a cooling breeze. The world is clean and quiet, and the scent of salt hangs pungent in the air. The water's vast surface is broken by tendrils of grassy marsh. It is the mighty Chesapeake, America's greatest estuary, whose shores gave birth to the nation's first settlements. It is the bay. It's not so deep, nor is it very wide; but it is big, and it has moods. It can be calm as glass—a haven for weekend pleasure boaters from Baltimore and Washington. But when it has a mind, it can conjure up squalls to quail the heart of the toughest skipper and make him run for cover. And it is generous: The bay yields up some of the continent's richest catches of seafood, valued at more than a hundred million dollars a year. Those who harvest this treasure are called watermen.

From the air, Smith Island looks less like an island and more like a series of fragile, grassy strands coiled for protection against the eroding bay. Clinging to the edge of these strands, as if held in place by spit and prayer, lie three tiny communities: Ewell, Rhodes Point, and Tylerton. Among them they contain five hundred and fifty souls, the island's total population and its most valuable resource. Right now, practically the entire population of Smith Island has only one thing in mind, and it will stay that way until late September. Crawling and swimming along the bottom of the bay, fighting, eating, and mating by the millions, are some of the Lord's most vicious, faithful, tricky, courageous, and baffling creatures, as well as one of God's greatest gastronomic gifts to man: Atlantic blue crabs. The warm weather has come, and they've crawled out of the mud, their winter's hibernation ended.

3

4

Since long before dawn the boats have been moving on the water. Although the average depth of the bay is only twenty-one feet, these watermen will be working in much shallower depths not far from shore. Their boats are barcats: small, one-man craft with flat bottoms that displace no more than eighteen inches of water. They can float in the very shallowest spots, right over mud and sandbars where the eel grass grows thickest and the crabs are most abundant. They are perfect for hand scraping. These watermen are after peelers, crabs that are about to shed their shells and become soft-shell crabs, the bay's most highly prized delicacy. But getting them to market is a long, hard process, and scraping them off the bottom is only the first part.

A hand scrape is an iron armature tapering at one end to a point, to which is attached a line. The other end flares out to form a three-and-a-half-foot open rectangle. To this is attached the nylon net, or bag. The hand scrapers are allowed by law to use two scrapes per boat, one on each side. When he arrives at his chosen spot, the waterman drops his scrapes into the water while he moves his boat at a moderate speed. They sink to the bottom because of their weight. The forward movement of the boat insures that the bag attached to the scrape will billow out and not get fouled up. Now the lower bar of the scrape bumps along the bottom, scraping off clumps of eel grass and, in the grass, crabs that are pulled back into the bag. Judgment and experience decide how long the scrapes should be dragged. The

watermen call this "makin' a lick." Here and there, some boats have stopped as the men start pulling in the scrapes, hand over hand. First comes the line, then the scrape, which is pulled over a man's head and behind his shoulders so he can get at the last part, the bag. The scrape weighs fifty pounds. The bag, depending on how full it is with mud, eel grass, and—one hopes—lots of crabs, may weigh up to three times that. This is work for a man with stamina and a strong back. Next begins the culling process. The contents of the bag are emptied onto a culling table, where the waterman quickly sorts through the mess he's dragged off the bottom and tosses his crabs into bushel containers around him. What is not usable gets shoved back in the water and the entire sequence begins again.

But beneath the boats—what's happening there? Crabs grow by a process called molting, or the periodic throwing off of their old, external skeletons. The watermen call this peeling, or shedding. It is known that when a blue crab begins to shed, it heads for the thickest eel grass it can find. Molting weakens the crab, and when its shell is soft, it is totally defenseless. What it needs is a safe place to hide while its new shell hardens and it regains its strength. The eel grass provides good camouflage.

The bay is a vast school that does not easily yield up its secrets. How does a man know where to fish for crabs? There are different kinds of bottom in the water. There's hard bottom and soft bottom. There's bottom that has tree stumps in it, from a time when Smith Island was much bigger, before a large part of the land was sucked into the bay. Each area has a good time and a bad time for crabs. A waterman has to learn where to go and when to go there if he wants a good catch.

By noon, without a cooling breeze, it has become hot on the water. The barcats' skippers have unfurled their boats' awnings to protect them from the sun. Soon it must be decided when to return to shore. Although their peeler and soft-shell crabs are being kept moist and covered in their containers, in their weakened state too much heat can kill them.

A waterman spends almost as much time in his crab shanty as he does on his boat because this is where he gets his crabs ready for market. A shanty is a shed built over water that holds the floats in which peelers are kept until they become soft-shell crabs.

A year ago, Carroll Marsh decided he was getting too old to pull scrapes, so he and his younger brother became partners. The brother catches the crabs while Carroll looks after their shanty and the business end of things.

It's one-thirty under a scorching sun when Marsh's brother noses his boat alongside the shanty walkway in Rhodes Point. Carroll hurries down to help unload the boat. Then he quickly carries the bushel baskets of crabs into the shade of the shed and puts the peeler crabs into floats. Each float is a four-by-eight-foot container into which is constantly pumped up to six inches of fresh water from the bay. The peeler crabs are separated into two categories. The rank crabs are those whose big fin is rimmed with bright red and, in a day or two, will molt and become soft-shells.

The green crabs are those whose big fin has a clear white sign. They must be kept longer until they, too, become rank and shed. If they were put together with the ranks, they would devour them as soon as their shells became soft. It isn't that the blue crab is a dedicated cannibal; it's more a matter of not turning away from an easy meal. "But what," some may ask, "is so special about a soft-shell crab?" Aside from the fact that it may be eaten whole, shell and claws and all, the answer lies only in the tasting.

Crabs are generous in providing information about their sex and physical growth. A male crab, called a jimmy, wears a long, shaftlike apron on his abdomen. A sook is a sexually mature female that has molted for the last time. She wears a wide, dome-shaped apron, and her claw tips are a bright red. She is capable of laying two million eggs, but perhaps only one in a million will produce an adult crab.

In most other respects, crabs are not so obliging. Tending the floats is practically a full-time job in itself. Timing is crucial. If a soft-shell crab is not fished up and refrigerated soon after it has shed, its new shell will become hard again within two hours and it will have to be thrown away as useless. Some watermen regard their peelers as babies. Often, in the process of shedding its old shell, a crab will get hung up and need help to get out. To watch the metamorphosis is to observe one of nature's great wonders. Imagine if humans, when they grew tired of their old and sagging skins, could just cast them off and emerge with a newly soft and youthful covering. Sadly, they cannot.

Praise the Lord! What a fine mornin'!"

It's five A.M., the sun's just slipped above the water, and he's hauling up the first scrape of the day. Charlie Marsh is in a good mood. He usually is. A pillar of his Methodist church, a man "who has a friendly association with God," Charlie, like other watermen past middle age, decided to give his back a break and rig a boat with a hydraulic scrape. His boat, the *Skimmer*, carries a mast and boom and is much deeper hulled than a barcat. He must fish in deeper water, where the eel grass is less abundant and there are fewer crabs. But Charlie's not complaining. He's grateful to go on working.

His foot presses the hydraulic power pedal while his hands guide the lifting bag to his culling table. He unloads the mess and, like a kid with both hands in a cookie jar, begins sorting through it.

Boats rigged with hydraulic lifts are allowed to use only one scrape, but these are bigger and heavier than those used by the hand scrapers. Most watermen agree that they are less effective than the hand scrapes. Since they are towed by two lines instead of one, they tend to angle upward when dragged along the bottom. Therefore, more crabs can get away. Nevertheless, for the older waterman who wants to keep on scraping, hydraulics is a new lease on life.

Marsh wears heavy gloves as he works. They look as though they've been through a war and, in a sense, they have. Crabs don't like being picked up, and a well-placed slash of their sharp claws can cut through work gloves and puncture a man's skin. Most watermen's hands are marked by scars.

There is an exact procedure in culling. Each crab Charlie Marsh finds is quickly held up to the light and examined for its sign. If the big fin shows a clear sign, it's a green. If a pink or red sign, it's a rank crab. Both are peelers, and these are what he's after. He breaks the claws of the crabs before tossing them into containers. Now, they won't be able to injure one another. Crabs that have no sign at all are thrown back into the water. These are not yet ready to molt. Maybe next week they will be. Sometimes he comes up with a big, hard-shell jimmy crab. There's a market for these, too, and they are tossed into a separate basket.

With a sharp eye, Marsh judges the size of his crabs while he's culling. The minimum legal size for a peeler is three inches. Anything smaller must be thrown back in the bay. When he's unsure, he checks the crab's size against a notched measuring stick at hand.

Lick after lick, the bushel baskets fill, and it's easy to see that Charlie Marsh is a happy man. From time to time he pulls a black rock out of the muck on his culling table and throws it onto the deck. What's this? During a pause in the work, he picks one up and pries into it with a knife, his eyes crinkling. Moist, gleaming, and succulent—a Chesapeake Bay oyster, the sweetest in the world! Some rocks. They never taste like these in a restaurant.

By twelve-thirty, Marsh eases behind the steering wheel of his cabin and has lunch: a couple of cheese sandwiches on white bread washed down with a can of Pepsi and followed by a handsome dose of strong coffee out of a thermos. It's still reasonably cool on the water, and he feels he can safely scrape for another hour or so. He figures a good day's haul will consist of four to five hundred crabs. He's not too far from that now. After expenses, he'll come out with maybe a hundred dollars for his day's work—and that'll do him just fine.

The last job every skipper does before turning his boat toward home is to wash and scrub clean his culling table and deck. Apart from the awful smell if he doesn't, the stuff from the bottom will dry and stick like glue.

Charlie Marsh secures his boat alongside his crab shanty and starts to unload his catch. He's got about two more hours of work before he can relax a bit. After putting his new crabs into their respective floats and throwing away the dead ones, with a dip net he fishes up all his newly shed soft-shell crabs and packs them neatly, according to size, into trays. The trays are covered with shaved ice and eel grass and packed into shipping boxes. The boxes are then placed in his shanty refrigerator. Tomorrow morning he'll put them on his walkway, where they'll be picked up long after he's gone crabbing, and taken to Crisfield on the mainland.

Over at Charlie's house, Mrs. Marsh has been preparing supper. Watermen eat early. Five is normal for their evening meal. A little before four, Charlie comes home, washes up, and sinks gratefully into his easy chair in the living room. At this point, he's been up and working for more than twelve hours. His head nods and he's in deep sleep almost instantly. His wife will wake him for supper. After that, he's conducting a Bible-study class in his home, and after that, he'll go down to his crab shanty to fish up the soft-shells once more. Next his bath, then bed will come at nine.

Smith Island's a fine place for kids to grow up. They're safe to wander and play wherever they like, though parents sometimes get a little nervous when the younger ones fool around down by the docks. But there's usually someone nearby to see that they don't fall in the water. For the older boys, the island is fun and adventure. They can borrow one of their daddies' small skiffs and, with a crew of pals and a dip net, pole around in shallow water for the crabs that got away.

Clustered as if for protection, around the sides of the island's churches lie the graves of the faithful. Smith Islanders respect their dead and intend to hang on to them. For this reason, each grave is covered with a heavy carved stone. The island's highest elevation is only five feet above sea level. In a hurricane or a bad storm, flooding is severe and people don't want to see caskets floating into the bay.

A waterman's average yearly income is about twelve thousand dollars. In most of America, such an income would be considered poverty level, and rightly so, especially after deductions for expenses and taxes. Yet there is no true poverty here. Smith Islanders are proud, independent people who would freeze at the thought of a free handout. Most people here own their own homes. In the past, houses were covered with white clapboard. Now, they wear white aluminum siding. And the houses, while nothing fancy, are neat as a pin, inside and out. The small interiors are spotless and comfortable, and the kitchens are designed for action. And, of course, just about everyone owns a color TV. During the week, the clothing worn is neat and functional, and on Sundays—well—folks look simply handsome. And Smith Islanders are well fed, maybe *too* well fed. How do they do it? As one lady comments, "It's because we're the world's best dollar stretchers." She's not fooling, though that isn't the entire story.

With the Island's biggest population, Ewell supports two grocery and general stores: Ruke's and LeRoy Evans's. They sell staples like milk, eggs, fresh meat, and canned goods. In the summer, there are usually fresh tomatoes, a few heads of hard lettuce, and maybe some carrots. Potatoes are available—and that's about it. Prices are higher than they are on the mainland: The stock has to be carried over by boat, and that costs money. But the stores perform another valuable service. They are also social gathering places for the watermen.

Evenings in Ewell are a pleasant time as compared to earlier in the day, when it is usually hot and soggy in summer. In the evening, after supper, those who have a little time will walk down the road to Ruke's, where there's a nice big screened room in the back, or they'll just sit on the porch and talk. And when two or more watermen meet, what do they talk about? That's right: crabs. Where they are and where they ain't. Are they movin' or ain't they? Is the market goin' up, down, or is it stayin' the same? And the thorny question: Should we cut out the middlemen, make our own co-op, and sell our crabs direct?

Something is missing here, but it's hard to define. Then it registers: Even in the heat of argument, no one's voice is raised in anger. Not a single "hell" or "damn" or other words that go bang in the night are to be heard here, or anywhere else on the island, or on the water. These people just don't swear! In the back room at LeRoy Evans's, it's the same way. There's lots of laughter. Men speak warmly but listen carefully, even to opposing points of view, because you never can tell when you might learn something worthwhile.

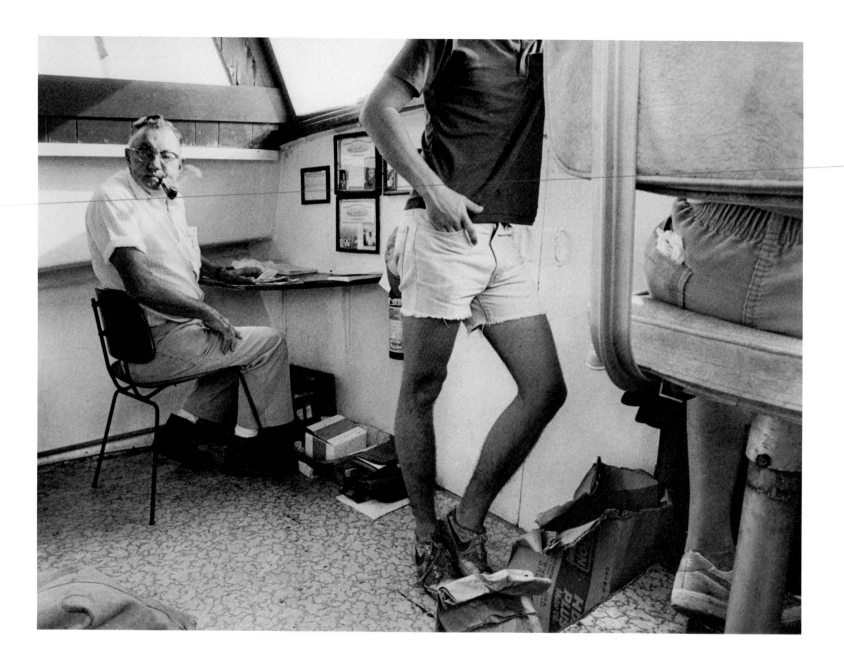

Sometimes, Frank Dize threatens to sell out and retire. "Too much work, never enough money, and worry, worry, worry all the time," he growls with an impish grin.

Of course, no one takes him seriously. If Frank Dize retired, Smith Island wouldn't be the same. Besides, what on earth would he do with himself? Nobody who knows him would argue that he is not a colorful man: small of stature, spare of frame, his pipe forever clamped between his teeth, his skin the color of red mahogany, always smiling, and always with something pleasant to say—when he isn't running.

As one of his neighbors puts it, "I reckon if Frank wanted to, he'd do just fine as one of them politic fellers over to the mainland. Why, he can talk so sweet, he can make the peelers shed before their time. And *that* ain't easy."

Perhaps this isn't quite true, but there's no denying that the man has charm.

Frank Dize is captain of the *Island Belle II*, the U.S. mail boat that services Smith Island to Crisfield on the eastern shore. His boat is a major link to the mainland, and his responsibilities are awesome. He carries the watermen's soft-shell crabs to Crisfield, where they are sold and shipped to the big cities. He hauls food, freight, supplies, and passengers twice a day, every day. On Sundays he makes only one crossing. He is a mobile banker for Ewell and Rhodes Point. Those with money to deposit in Crisfield give it to Frank, who makes the deposits for them. Not only must he keep all the records straight, but if anything should happen to this money, he is responsible for it.

Frank employs his son and grandson, who are his crew on the *Island Belle II*. By six-thirty in the morning, they're both hard at work. One by boat and the other by truck, they go through Ewell and Rhodes Point collecting the soft-shell crab boxes stacked outside the watermen's crab shanties. Then they return to the *Island Belle II* and start loading the boxes on board.

By seven-thirty A.M., Frank Dize is half-walking, half-running toward his battered Chevy, having finished his usual breakfast: one cup of coffee. He's heading for Rhodes Point to pick up the mail there and the mail from Tylerton as well. Tylerton is separated from the rest of Smith Island by a channel of water, so Frank has an arrangement with a man who ferries the mail back and forth by boat. Now, he turns back toward Ewell, picking up boat passengers on the way and the mail at Ewell's tiny post office.

At eight-thirty, sharp, the *Island Belle II* casts off its lines and gets under way. There's a good complement of passengers on board. Frank goes around shaking hands, chucking babies under their chins, and patting the cheeks of pretty women. Frank has an eye for the ladies. His wife, Barbara, knows it. "Lookin' and talkin' don't do much," she observes dryly.

But now, it's down to business as Dize settles into a chair in front of a corner-hung desktop in the wheelhouse. He leaves the running of the boat to his son Frankie and grandson Jamie and turns to his endless accounts, bills of money, scribbled slips of paper heaped before him. Not even the shapely legs of a girl perched on top of the wheelhouse can distract him.

On top of everything else, Frank's got to keep track of each crab box on board his boat. He must write down the names of the watermen who are sending them to market, the quantity, the size of the crabs in each box, and the buyers who will be picking them up in Crisfield. It's enough to make a man dizzy, but these boxes are essential to the economy of Smith Island, and the watermen like to send their crabs with Frank. Not only is he dependable, but his boat's fast. She can make the crossing in thirty-five minutes. That's important when you're handling perishable goods.

Soon, the outline of Crisfield, Maryland, comes into view. The boat takes a heading toward the long county dock, where most commercial vessels tie up. Here there are trucks, pickups, and UPS vans waiting. Even before the passengers have disembarked, Frankie and Jamie are working like demons to unload the crab boxes. Other hands snatch them up to load into the waiting vehicles. Tonight, some of the finest restaurants in Baltimore, Washington, New York, and perhaps even Boston will enjoy this remarkable delicacy: soft-shell crabs.

During the lull that follows, Frank Dize, money bags in hand, steps off his boat and strides briskly toward town to make his rounds. His first stop is at the big hardware store two streets up. Here he orders spare parts, supplies, and equipment for some of the watermen back on the island. Yes, Frank is also a purchasing agent. Whatever he orders will be sent down to his boat before his return trip. The tricky part is, Frank's got to pay for it, right on the spot, out of his own pocket, because no one's given him any money yet.

Next stop's a big one: the bank. Dize carefully unloads and slips thick wads of bills onto the counter in front of the teller's window. He keeps her occupied for a while. Isn't it strange that in all his years, no one's tried to mug or rob him? "People 'round here just don't do things like that, sonny," he replies, almost with a straight face. Nevertheless, he is visibly more relaxed when leaving the premises.

It's time for lunch. Even *he* must eat sometime. It's his usual no-nonsense place, featuring its usual no-nonsense food. About halfway through the meal, Frank's already paid his bill, is looking at his watch, takes a gulp of coffee, and after a big good-bye wave and grin, is gone. The man is fast.

35

Tom's Barbershop is in the same direction he's going. He decides there's enough time for a quick visit. It's a favorite haunt of mature and retired watermen. One of the latter is receiving a trim in Tom's barber chair. There is only one of these in the shop. Frank engages in a lively conversation with an old friend. The two seated men can see their reflections in a large, ornately framed-in-oak mirror on the opposite wall. It's cool in here, a welcome refuge from the heat outside and a nice place to visit. But the *Island Belle II* leaves at twelve-thirty and Frank's got to go.

Down at the dock, a new array of vehicles now stands opposite the boat, and all sorts of goods and foodstuffs are being loaded on board. There's just enough room left for the passengers.

Back at Smith Island, the freight, mail, and empty crab boxes are unloaded and delivered by Frankie and Jamie. Meanwhile, Frank goes around to the people who ordered merchandise and tries to collect the money he's laid out for them. Sometimes they can't pay him right away. Then it's back to the boat for the second trip of the day and the same procedure all over again.

After supper, Frank sits at a small desk in his bedroom writing down his final accounts of the day. In spite of all those figures in his head, he rarely makes a mistake, but all this juggling is bound to produce some side effects. As Barbara Dize says, "Frank's real good in public. You don't never see him gettin' short with nobody. It's when he comes home he lets it out, and I can't truly fault him for it. Frank's a good man," she adds. "He just don't know how to relax, and if he did, he wouldn't have the time."

They call it the highway—a thin stretch of bumpy asphalt that connects Ewell to Rhodes Point. It's about a mile and a half long, and this is where Smith Island automobiles come to die. For a hundred yards or more, both sides of the road are strewn with the corpses of abandoned cars begging for a decent burial. But there is no help in sight. When people need an automobile, they go to the mainland, where they pick out a reasonable used vehicle and have it towed over to the island on a barge. That sometimes costs almost as much as the car does. Then, if they get two or three years' use out of it, they figure they're ahead. After that, it's countdown time. No automobile can survive the island's moist, corrosive, salt air much longer. Some undercarriages look like they've been riddled by machine-gun fire. Then what's to be done with a car that has died? Towing it off the island would be too costly, and burying it wouldn't work, because the soil's too thin. In an attempt to soften the harsh reality, some call this place Smith Island's modern art museum—no admission charged.

From the age of six, boys start going out on their daddies' boats during the crabbing season. By the time they are teenagers, most are becoming knowledgeable watermen. But what do teenagers do on a Saturday night on Smith Island? There are no movie houses here. No discos, bowling alleys, Pizza Huts or McDonald's.

Harry's Place in Ewell is a popular hangout for the younger kids. They can buy ice cream, or burgers and fries and Coke. There's a back room with a couple of pool tables and a few electronic arcade games. All innocent fun. But some of the older boys have other ideas. Throughout the night they'll be coasting up and down the highway in their jalopies, tape machines blaring rock music, getting high on alcohol and drugs. Girls, too. Drugs and alcohol have never been sold on Smith Island, not even beer. They come from the mainland, along with the itch to use them. And now, Smith Island's hurting, too, in a way that the rest of America knows only too well.

Saturday night is also a night for softball games at Ewell's Eddie Evans Baseball Diamond. The field's only five years old, but it gets lots of use. There are plenty of teenagers here and a good crowd in general. Tonight's game features the Jimmies versus the Buckrams. The teams always adopt crab names. It's fun watching these watermen play. Where they find the time to practice is anyone's guess, but they're good and the game's full of action. Wives scream encouragement to husbands on the field. Old men hoot at the visiting team's folly. Kids sip soda pop, their eyes glued to the field, and over the public-address system rolls the rich, baritone voice of Jennings Evans delivering his usual scintillating commentary on the game. Who won? You'll never find out.

There's a new preacher on the island and she's a woman. Reverend Janet Rounsley stepped off of Frank Dize's boat and entered a world unlike any she had known before. That was six days ago. This morning, she's going to preach the first Sunday sermon in her new ministry. Well, three sermons, actually: one for each community. Is she nervous? You bet. So are some of the people in her congregation. No one walks around carrying a cross, but Smith Islanders take their religion seriously. It's the touchstone of their lives. They're also fair-minded people. If this new lady preacher is good for their church and their island, there'll be no problem. And if she isn't? They've lived with bad preachers before and survived.

Meanwhile, the lady in question has completed her first service in Ewell's church, been whisked off in a pickup to Rhodes Point and helped into a small boat for the crossing to Tylerton. Janet Rounsley has a real fear of being on small boats, but the waterman who conducted her later reported, "Couldn't see nor a sign of it from her." Next, the service in Tylerton and the return passage over the water. Here, she finally addresses the congregation at Rhodes Point, her last service of the day. She's a bit frazzled, unused to the island's heat and humidity, but as she speaks, any lingering doubts about her begin to vanish. Her address is, more than anything else, an expression of deep gratitude to the people of the island who have so lovingly welcomed her and her husband, Bill, also a preacher. She expresses her wonder at a place where no one bothers to lock their doors, because no one covets their neighbors' property. She plans to learn all she can about the island's needs and problems so that she may give her help where it is needed.

Lynette Hoffman, nearing eighty, plays the organ during a period of silent prayer. Then Reverend Rounsley asks for two people to come and sing a song for everyone. Elizabeth Evans and Holly Bradshaw go up to the altar and, with help from the organ, sing "Thanks to Calvary."

Reverend Rounsley gives the blessing, and suddenly the service is ended. There is no doubting the warmth of those who stop for a word and to shake her hand as they leave the church. The new preacher's going to do just fine.

On Monday morning, it's crabs as usual. A little before four A.M., the night's blackness is shattered as light bulbs are turned on in crab shanties all along the waterfront. It's fishing-up time for the softs. Some watermen have built their floats out in the open, beyond their shanties. That's what Bill Dize did. The theory is that direct sunlight on the water in the floats will make the peelers shed faster. Fewer mortalities are also claimed. "Maybe," opponents respond. "But who wants to keep fightin' off gulls with bottomless gullets, lots of nerve, and nothin' but time on their feathers?" Bill Dize leaves his short-tempered, nimble dog, Blackie, to roam around his floats while he's gone. He suffers few losses.

At a quarter to five, he guides his boat, *Sally*, slowly through Ewell's water thoroughfare. Lights still shine in shanties along the banks. Here and there men greet each other softly, then go on to their day's work. Some watermen won't leave Ewell for a while longer. They'll be working close to home. But Bill's got a ways to go. He'll be scraping in Virginia waters today—south, "across the border." He knows these waters well. He should. He's a born Tangier man, raised and learned the water from his daddy on Tangier Island, seven miles south of Smith, but in Virginia. For a long time, there's been fierce rivalry—and some trouble, too—between Virginia and Maryland watermen. The laws of territoriality were amended, and tensions have settled down. Bill met and married a nice Smith Island girl, but he still gets the longing to scrape in Virginia waters. He's had to buy two crabbing licenses, one from each state: They both want a piece of the action.

Every waterman knows that the bay is in danger, not from them, but from the dumping of industrial and other wastes into its waters. It's hard to get politicians to move when there are conflicting interests involved. Heavy industry provides jobs and pumps up the economy. The watermen are a small, isolated group about whom most people know little or nothing. Few who enjoy their product make the connection between what they do and the sizable industry that, without *them*, could not exist. But what's remarkable is that, in spite of all the pollution in Chesapeake Bay, the crabs are thriving. Do they know something we don't? Bill Dize believes, "They're a heck of a lot smarter than we are. They're survivin' in conditions that are killin' off other creatures down there and would sure enough finish *us* off. I'd call that smart, and the proof is, there's as many crabs now as there's been in the last fifteen years."

51

Scraping is not the only way to catch crabs. Another way is to trap them in a device called a crab pot.

The mist this morning is like a white shroud, blanketing the sky and the water. How can anybody find a small marker buoy bobbing on the water in this? Ed Evans steers the *Susan Leighann* alongside the first of his many strings of crab pots and halts the boat. His son, Glenn, springs into action, gaffs the line under the buoy, and hauls the pot on the other end on board, where he passes it to his father. Evans opens the top of the pot, turns it upside down, shakes out the crabs onto his culling table, and hands the pot back to his son to be thrown back into the water. But wait. Why has he left a crab inside? "Why, it's a male jimmy and he's the bait. How else you gonna catch females in a pot? You throw this feller down there, pretty soon them sex-hungry she-crabs'll start sniffin' 'round that jimmy. Next thing, they'll be crawlin' in that pot. Once they're in, they ain't comin' out 'til we shake 'em out."

Speed is important in this work. The more efficiently a captain and his crew work as a team, the more pots they can put out in the water. More pots mean more crabs. The pots are laid out in a string that may number up to fifty. They are not connected to one another. Each pot functions as a separate unit with a nylon line attached to the pot on the bottom and, at the other end, to a distinctive marker buoy that floats on the surface for owner identification. Each string is laid out in as straight a line as possible to minimize the time it takes for the boat to reach the next buoy and for a crewman to haul that pot out of the water. And so it goes. When you've set out five hundred pots as Evans has, you've got to work fast. There's a small grin on his face as he turns the boat around toward home. He's had a good morning. Suddenly, his son, Glenn, springs to the stern and starts throwing brand-new pots in the water while the boat cruises along. What's going on? There are no jimmies in these pots. " 'Course not," Evans explains. "Them pots is for peelers." Don't you need bait for them? "Peelers got other things on their minds. They're lookin' for protection while they're sheddin'." And the pots give them a place to hide until they're strong again? "That's it. Only we don't give 'em the chance, poor devils."

For those who scrape near shore, high August can be a misery. Hordes of gnats, green flies, and mosquitoes torment everything that moves in or around the marshlands. The potters who go after hard-shell jimmies have their own troubles. They work in deeper waters where August is the time to look out for algae blooms, colonies of millions of micro-organisms fed by the dumping of fertilizer wastes from farms into the upper bay. They drift, and when they die, they absorb and destroy the oxygen in the water, killing all marine life in their path. Watermen have hauled up entire strings of pots, only to find dead crabs inside. Then there are the sea nettles, a kind of jellyfish—no end of them in the water. Pull up a pot and it's swarming with the slimy things. Where they touch a man's flesh, it burns like fire. If they catch an

54

eye, it can stop a man's work for a while. These are the hazards of the trade.

Soft-shell crabs are sold by the dozen and command a price five times higher than the hard-shells. But there's a market for the hards as well. The catch is, they're sold by the bushel, so a waterman's got to catch more of them. The biggest number-one jimmies and the larger number twos are sold live to markets along the East Coast. They'll be served up in crab houses and seafood restaurants. The females are in demand in oriental communities, where it is believed that their flesh is sweeter than the males'. All other hard-shells are sold to the picking houses, mostly in Crisfield. The crabs are placed in metal containers and steamed. Then, seated on both sides of long tables, women tear off the backs, crack open the shells, and, with knives, pick out the cooked crab meat. The meat is packed, refrigerated, and sold to eager buyers. And everyone's happy. Or almost.

Smitty Smith is captain of the *C C Rider* out of Rhodes Point. He's a potter, going for hard-shell jimmies. He loves his work, but for almost two weeks he's been fretting. The picking houses in Crisfield have all the hard-shell crabs they can handle. Buyers also claim that there's less interest in the big jimmies now. Prices are dropping fast. "Normally," says Smith, "I'll get twenty, maybe twenty-five dollars for a nice bushel of number ones. Say I come up with thirty-five bushels a day. At regular prices, a man can live on that. Now they're offerin' fifteen, even twelve dollars a bushel. It don't make sense."

He's right. Potting for hard-shell crabs requires a crew. One man can't do the work alone. Smith employs two able teenage boys. They must be paid. He must buy bait for his pots every day: menhaden, herring, or bluefish, when he can get it. Hard-shell crabs like fresh fish and they are big eaters. Then there is fuel. The pots, of course, are not free, nor is all the nylon line that's used. A crab pot's life expectancy used to be just one season. Not too long ago, watermen learned that by fixing zinc bars to the bottom of a pot, they could get an extra year out of it. Zinc attracts saltwater corrosion away from the pot's iron mesh and so prolongs its life—a new wrinkle to do a job better. But what's a man to do when his deck is loaded with crabs and selling them will barely cover his expenses?

The following day, Smitty Smith runs the *C C Rider* over to the boat railway at Rhodes Point. Great slings are fastened around the boat's hull, and it is hoisted out of the water by a huge hydraulic lift that then wheels it onto dry land.

"The boat needs a good scrapin' and a new paint job. Might as well do it now," explains Smith. "Who knows? Crab prices might go up again any day."

There are many ways to prepare crabs for the table. Give a waterman his choice and he'll ask for stewed jimmies every time. Once tasted, the memory of this dish will start the juices flowing. But in order to eat a jimmy, you must first pick him up. He might not like that. A six-inch male hard-shell crab is a fierce antagonist, ready to attack opponents many times his size when provoked. If you plan to come up behind him unawares, be careful. His eyes are on stalks that can be raised, lowered, or swiveled like a periscope. He can move with remarkable speed, and he has a very short temper. Scientists have established that he has a highly developed nervous system. Yes. But can he think? Watermen are forever debating this question. "I can't say for sure if they can think or not, but I sure wish they could talk," says one. "That ways we'd know where they is or ain't gonna be." "That'd be right smart," agrees another. "But how're we gonna know they was tellin' the truth?"

Cindy Smith has no interest in these matters. She lets her father-in-law pick up the jimmies out of his floats and, one by one, tear off their backs. If this be murder, she feels no guilt. Tonight, Captain Smith will dine on stewed jimmies with dumplings and gravy and corn on the cob and . . .

In spite of its low profile on the water, Smith Island possesses a special beauty. But one must seek it out. More than a third of the island's land mass is marshland, useless for human habitation but perfect for a wildlife refuge. Here live mink and otter, fox and muskrat. In the spring and summer, thousands of herons, egrets, and ibis build their nests. Here, too, the osprey, or fish hawk, is making a remarkable comeback; artificial nesting platforms have produced good results. At one point, this fine bird was close to extinction. In the fall, flocks of migrating waterfowl settle down for the cold season, both ducks and geese. For a short time then, it's open season for hunters. It's an important way, too, for Smith Islanders to stretch their tight budgets: They catch or hunt much of the food they eat. But Lord help any man who poaches out of season.

Mike K. Harrison, Sr., is not a man to cross lightly. He's the officer in charge of everything that happens in the refuge, and it's a big job. His current project involves banding black ducks so that their migration patterns may be studied. He catches the birds in wire traps baited with corn, then fishes them out with a net. Once in his hands, they are quiet and seem trusting, as though they know he won't harm them. When the band is securely fastened around the duck's foot, Mike hefts the duck gently into the air and it takes off, honking back to whatever ducks do for a living, no worse for wear.

63

For some Smith Islanders, growing old is a personal triumph. Just look at these two! He's . . . and she's. . . . Well, it's not nice to tell a lady's age. Enos and Marie Evans are married fifty years today!

In the basement of Ewell's church, it's standing room only. People have come from all over the island, and from the mainland, too, to share the celebration. There's even a telegram from the President, and it's not a request for more taxes. Up on the platform sits Reverend Rounsley next to Enos and Marie Evans, listening. And everybody else listens as Jennings Evans delivers one of his justly famed eulogies. The man is good. He might have made it in show biz, but the call of the water was too strong. There are some tears in the audience and plenty of laughter as Jennings delivers a running commentary on the couple's lives. He finishes to warm applause.

After more speakers, it's finally Ruke Dize's turn. Ruke gets up and, with hands clasped in true concert-hall fashion, sings a heartrending version of the Lord's Prayer. Now it's chow time. One entire wall is lined with tables loaded with food. Not common, garden-variety food, but Smith Island's finest. It may not be healthy, but no one's crazy enough *not* to eat it.

Dawn has come and gone. It's late morning and the scraping has been poor. Lick after lick yields mostly junk. "I sure hope them potters are havin' better luck. That's usually the way of it. When the scrapin's poor, the pottin's good and versa vice."

He's a great hulk of a man with a remarkably gentle disposition. All that work and not a single bushel basket filled. There is a rhythm in this work like the surging of the tides. He makes it look easy but it isn't.

Why do these men spend their lives at such back-wrenching toil for so little return? Barry Bruce tries to explain. "Oh," he sighs, "it's somethin' about bein' out there on that boat. On that water. And of a mornin', when you're goin' to work, and that sun's a comin' up and everything's still, and the water's just like you're ridin' on top of glass . . ."

Yes. There is a magic time on the water between night and day that is like no other, when the world seems to hold its breath.

The gulls hover about him, almost close enough to touch, as he works through the mound on his culling table. "They don't bother me none," he says. "We got an understandin'. They don't mess with my crabs and I let 'em feed off of what's left."

He holds a clump of eel grass aloft. In it are embedded tiny shrimp. Immediately, the gulls dart in, deftly picking out the treat. Then they back off politely, still hovering alongside the barcat.

"See?" He smiles. "They're good company."

But it's been an unprofitable morning. It would be pointless to continue. Bruce glances ruefully at his catch and says, "Oh, well. 'Least there's enough so's the missus can fix us a nice supper."

Whatare all the women doing? For two weeks, every housewife on Smith Island has been cleaning and scrubbing, washing and mending, sewing and painting, cooking and baking, all with fatiguing intensity. Why this do-or-die crusade? "Well, for heaven's sake. Camp meetin's comin'!" What's that? "Why, it's the most important to-do on this island!" And so it is.

Every August since 1896, camp meetings have been held on Smith Island. They last a week, from Sunday to Sunday. Their original purpose was to revive people's faith and to win new souls for Jesus. That hasn't changed. But now, there is an additional function served. Camp meetings are also a time of reunion. Many friends and relatives who have left Smith Island return, and, for this one week, live and worship with their own once more.

Behind Ewell's church is a large, shedlike structure with open sides. This is the tabernacle where the meetings take place. Outside, people move from group to group, greeting old friends, all of them dressed in their finest. Babies not seen before are fussed over and cooed at. It's a day off for the watermen, but in spite of the occasion, wherever they group together talk invariably turns to crabs. Some of the older visitors study the church's gravestones with interest. There is history in these engraved names—Guy, Sneade, Somers, Dize, Evans—names that trace back to the seventeenth century and the men who sailed with Captain John Smith, the great English explorer who discovered Chesapeake Bay. "Wondrous faire and delightsome," he called it then. That judgment has stood the test of time.

The first service of the day is about to begin. All enter the tabernacle. This is a testimony meeting, an old church tradition. Individual members of the congregation rise and, moved by personal emotion or conviction, testify, or relate their own spiritual experiences. A waterman stands. "I bless Jesus every day for keepin' me safe and fit on that water. I ain't ever forgettin' what He does for me." Amens are murmured in recognition. A young woman rises, tears in her eyes. "My Aunt June, she's got cancer. She's not so old but the doctors say there's no cure. Blessed Jesus, if you're gonna take her, don't let her suffer, Lord. Please, don't let her suffer." There is prayer now. The congregation as one, in support of this request. A spritely old lady jumps to her feet and says, "I just want to testify how fine I feel every day. I feel the spirit movin' in me an', if it's your will, Lord, maybe you'll let me stay in this nice place a little longer. Thank you, Lord. Bless you. Amen."

Sunday service is held following the testimony meeting. Emotions are running high today. A long wooden bench has been placed at the foot of the platform to serve as an altar. Those who wish to be anointed with oil and to pray for themselves or for others, are encouraged to come forward. An elderly woman comes and kneels in front of the altar, sobbing. Reverend Rounsley rushes to her side to comfort her and join her in prayer. On the platform, Bill Rounsley raises his arms and leads the congregation in song.

Who can doubt their sincerity? Their faith and devotion shine on their faces. This sustains them, and not just during camp meetings or Sunday services. It can be seen daily in the way they conduct their lives.

After supper, there is an evening service. A gifted young evangelist from Georgia has come to preach the sermon. Before he speaks, there is singing, and the words ring sweetly in the evening air:

"Amazing Grace, how sweet the sound
that saved a wretch like me.
I once was lost but now am found,
was blind, but now I see.

'Twas Grace that taught my heart to fear
and Grace my fears relieved.
How precious did that Grace appear
the hour I first believed."